Surprise

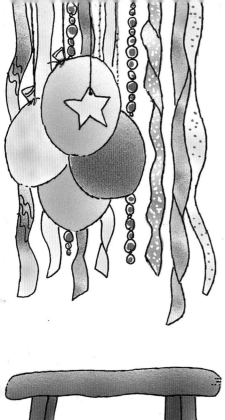

Knock, knock!
Who is at the door?

2

Why, it is Squirrel.
Come in, Squirrel.
Here is your hat.
Here is your whistle.

5

Knock, knock!
Who is at the door?

6

Why, it is Mouse.
Come in, Mouse.
Here is your hat.
Here is your whistle.

Knock, knock!
Who is at the door?

10

Why, it is Rabbit.
Come in, Rabbit.
Here is your hat.
Here is your whistle.

Knock, knock!
Who is at the door?

14

Why, it is Frog.
Come in, Frog.
Here is your hat.
Here is your whistle.

Knock, knock!
Who is at the door?
Is it Cat?
Get your hats.
Get your whistles.

18

Surprise!

It is not Cat.
It is Dog.
Here comes Cat now.

22

Surprise!
Happy birthday, Cat!

24